The Marshmallowist

Oonagh Simms
Additional text by Jenny Simms
Photography by Helen Cathcart
Square Peg, London

To my family, for always letting me be whatever I wanted to be (even when I was 4, and I wanted to be a dog)

As The Marshmallowist I like to do things differently. My marshmallows have surprising flavour pairings and a bright, fresh twist. I trained as a chocolatier in Paris, then went on to sell my marshmallows from a market stall on London's Portobello Road, combining classic techniques with unique, inspired flavour adventures.

In this book I share my secret for creating perfect marshmallows – both classic and vegetarian – and irresistible recipes using them in unexpected ways, drawn from the seasons.

Contents

Spring, Paris & Patisserie *page 22*

Summer, Friends & Outdoor Eating *page 48*

Autumn, London & Markets *page 80*

Winter, Home & Feasting *page 106*

Introduction

As a carefree teenager, craving to become a chocolatier and with a passion for patisserie, I decided to move to Paris. I did all the usual running-off-to-Paris things: moved into the top floor of a crumbling apartment block; borrowed a cat; perched precariously on the back of scooters… But I also enrolled at the CFA Médéric cookery school. Financing this by first working at (in fact, being almost sacked from) a bustling French bistro, then by managing a far-too-trendy fashion boutique, I was finally well on the way to achieving my sweet dream.

After four years of grindingly hard cooking: early mornings, countless black coffees, total bake-ache, 30,000 croissants, 10,000 profiteroles… and learning quite the rudest French swear words from perhaps the angriest *chef de partie* in the whole of Paris, I finally emerged, qualified as a fully trained *pâtissière* and *chocolatière*.

Ready for an adventure, I came to London to work for a leading luxury confectioner. And that's when I suddenly realised that something was missing… You see, in Paris I would make perhaps four different types of marshmallow a week. They'd be used in gateaux, brought along to dinner parties, or served as a petit four alongside a *café crème*. But in England? Here there were just those sad pink-and-white puffs that are only brought out to soak up the end of a bonfire…

Well, that just wouldn't do at all.

I wanted to create decadent marshmallows in grown-up flavours, with a French soufflé-like texture but a definite London edge. I experimented with flavours, sometimes unwisely (yes, that means you, lemon, olive oil and basil: bleurgh). Soon I had eight flavour combinations that I loved so much I could have written sonnets to them, if I could write sonnets: from a delicate Elderflower to an intense and fiery Passion Fruit & Ginger. I blagged myself a Saturday market stall on the world-famous Portobello Road and, from then on, I became The Marshmallowist.

I won't pretend it was an easy start. It was hard to find enough hours in the day to boil, whisk, cut, fluff and, most importantly, taste. So I eventually gave up my job, my London flat – and frankly, most of my social life – to dedicate myself to the craft. And I really believe there is a craft to mallow making. Each batch takes more than three days to perfect: they are whipped, left to set at just the right temperature, hand cut, then individually turned to ensure – well – perfection. In this book, I share some of my signature recipes and flavour combinations. Then, because I like the look of you, I'm going to throw in some of my favourite twists on classic desserts and treats: recipes that have been inspired by bustling markets, late-night feasting, parties in fields and – most of all – angry French chefs.

The Rules

Be careful not to over-whip your mallows or they will become dense and feel more like nougat, which is not the consistency you are looking for.

Make sure you take the purée to 115°C exactly. If you overheat the purée it will turn into jam, which makes the marshmallow dense. Overheating also removes the moisture, which will significantly impact the taste. If you overcook the purée, don't panic, just add a teacup of cold water to cool it down and reheat it to the magic 115°C.

Do line the tray with cling film and oil it thoroughly, otherwise the mixture will stick to the cling film and be impossible to remove.

Mix together the glucose and fruit purée in a stand mixer very thoroughly, or else when you pour out the finished marshmallow you will end up with wet layers in between the fluffy mixed mixture.

If the marshmallows are runny, check your sugar thermometer: you may not be boiling the mix to the right temperature (use my calibration technique, see page 10, for guidance).

For coating the set marshmallows I use a 50:50 mix of cornflour and icing sugar. The cornflour is pure starch and so absorbs the moisture from the outsides of the mallow. Using 100% cornflour wouldn't taste particularly great, while icing sugar on its own would be absorbed fully by the mallow, so the 50:50 mix gives you a happy compromise. If your marshmallows are a bit sticky, up the amount of cornflour.

Flavour Adventures

One of the great pleasures of making marshmallows is that their delicate texture allows you to play with flavour combinations in whatever way tickles your fancy. In this book I have pulled out some of my most popular (and my personal favourite) combinations as a guide. But treat them as that, simply as guides to help you to discover your own preferences. Playing with new tastes and pairing fruits with herbs, spices and even vegetables is how to become a true Marshmallowist.

The Basics

Fruit Purée

Makes 500ml

- 500g soft fruit (try strawberries or raspberries for your first time)
- 50g icing sugar
- 1 tbsp freshly squeezed lemon juice

1   Put the fruit in a blender (or use a hand-held blender) and whizz until puréed. Add the sugar and lemon juice and blend to combine (see below for ratios). Push through a sieve if you don't want the seeds. Leave to cool.

2   The purée can be covered and stored in the refrigerator for 1 week, or frozen for up to 3 months.

	Add straight to blender with lemon juice and 10% icing sugar to fruit	Peel, core or deseed, then simmer with 10% icing sugar to fruit and a little water until soft; use in the fruit purée recipe above
Creamy fruit (mango, banana, melon)	✓	
Exotic fruit (passion fruit)	✓	
Orchard Fruit (apples, pears)		✓
Root vegetables (pumpkin, sweet potatoes)		✓
Soft berries (strawberry, blackberry)	✓	
Stone fruit (peaches, plums, apricots)		✓

Whole Fruit Marshmallow

Makes 25 full-size (4.5cm square) marshmallows

Here is my signature recipe. Once you have mastered this, you can go on to create some of the other flavours in the book, or feel free to trundle off on your own flavour adventures.

Equipment:
25cm square baking tin
heavy-based saucepan
sugar thermometer
stand mixer
palette knife or spatula
sieve

○ flavourless vegetable oil, for the tin
○ 27g (13 leaves) gelatine
○ 300g granlated sugar
○ 190g Fruit Purée (see opposite; I suggest raspberry for your first time)
○ 250g icing sugar, mixed with 250g cornflour, for dusting

1   Line a 25cm square baking tin with cling film and use the oil to coat the film. In a microwaveable bowl, soak the gelatine in 300ml of cold water for 5 minutes. Wring out the gelatine gently to remove excess water (pour away any remaining water in the bowl). Return the gelatine to the bowl and heat in a microwave for about 1 minute, or until completely melted, but keep an eye on it and *do not let it boil* or it will lose its setting properties.

2   Put all the granulated sugar, 120ml of the glucose and 100g of the Fruit Purée into a heavy-based saucepan and place over a medium heat. Using a sugar thermometer in the saucepan, bring the mixture up to 115°C, stirring occasionally so it does not catch on the pan. Meanwhile, pour the remaining 90g of Fruit Purée and 120ml of glucose into the bowl of a stand mixer and gently whisk together on a very low speed.

3   When the mixture in the saucepan has reached 115°C, slowly pour the hot liquid in a slow, steady stream into the mixer, still running at a very low speed. Add the melted gelatine, then increase the speed to medium and whisk for 10 minutes. The marshmallow mixture will begin to firm up.

4   Once the marshmallow mix has tripled in volume and drops slowly off the whisk in thick ribbons, pour it into the prepared tin and smooth the top with a dampened palette knife or spatula. Dust the top of the mallows with some of the prepared sugar / cornflour mix, and leave to set at room temperature for 6 hours (or, even better, overnight) before cutting.

5   Dust a work surface with a nice thick layer of the icing sugar and cornflour dusting mix. Carefully tip the set marshmallow slab out of the tin, using the corners of the cling film to give you some lift. Dip a sharp knife in hot water to heat it, trim the edges of the marsh-mallow slab neatly, then cut into 4.5cm squares.

6   Toss the cut mallows into the bowl of dusting mix and fully coat. Put them in a sieve and gently shake off any excess dusting. They are now ready to be eaten, or will keep in an airtight container at room temperature for up to 3 weeks.

Vegetarian Marshmallows

Makes 36 x 3cm squares

Making vegetarian marshmallows is notoriously tricky. This is the only recipe I find to be successful with an easily acquired substitute for gelatine. Before you start, make sure that your stand mixer bowl is clean and dry and has no greasy residue (cleaning it with a small dab of white wine vinegar on kitchen paper works perfectly.)

Equipment:
20cm square baking tin
heavy-based saucepan
sugar thermometer
stand mixer
palette knife or spatula
sieve

- 250g icing sugar, mixed with 250g cornflour, for dusting
- 2tsp agar agar powder
- 200ml water
- 200g granlated sugar
- 100g glucose syrup
- 3 egg whites
- 1 tsp guar gum
- 1/4 tsp cream of tartar
- 2 tsp vanilla bean paste

1 Line a 20cm square baking tin with cling film and dust in a small portion of the 50/50 sugar/cornflour mix.

2 Dissolve the agar agar powder in 120ml of water in a small saucepan and leave to one side.

3 Mix together the sugar, glucose and 80ml of water in a pan and bring to the boil to make your sugar syrup. Cook the mixture until it reaches 120°C on a sugar thermometer.

4 Put the agar mixture on the heat, bring to the boil and cook for one minute, stirring constantly.

5 Combine the egg whites, guar gum, cream of tartar and vanilla and whip until stiff, usually about 4 minutes. Gently pour the sugar syrup in, keeping your mixture on a medium speed. Increase the speed, and continue to whip for 2 minutes.

6 Add in the cooked agar mix and beat for a further 12-15 minutes at full speed. The marshmallow mixture should be stiff and produce firm ribbons.

7 Pour into the tin and smooth with a damp palette knife. Leave to set overnight at room temperature.

8 Dust a work surface by sifting over a thick layer of the dusting mix. Tip the marshmallow slab out of the tin, using the cling film to give you some lift. Dip a sharp knife in hot water to heat it, trim the edges of the slab neatly, then cut into squares. Roll in dusting mix, then leave to dry for 24 hours before eating. Store in an airtight container at room temperature for up to 5 days.

Vanilla Bean Fluffed Marshmallow

(The American Classic)

This versatile fluff is used in many recipes throughout the book. It adds a soft marshmallow swirl to desserts, and is a creative alternative to cream or a butter cream for cake fillings.

Makes 2 large jam jars (about 400g)

- 150g granulated sugar
- large pinch of fine salt
- 170ml glucose
- 2 large egg whites, at room temperature
- ¼ tsp cream of tartar
- 1 tsp vanilla bean paste

1   Mix together the sugar, salt, glucose and 80ml of cold water in a small saucepan. Bring to the boil over a medium heat, stirring occasionally, until the mixture reaches 110°C on a sugar thermometer.

2   Meanwhile, place the egg whites and cream of tartar in the bowl of a stand mixer. Whisk, on medium speed, to soft peaks.

3   When the syrup has reached 110°C, reduce the speed of the mixer to very low and slowly pour 2 tbsp of syrup into the egg white mix. (This heats the mix, so avoids the eggs from scrambling in the hot syrup.) Increase the mixer speed to medium-high, slowly add the remaining syrup in a thin stream and whip the fluff until it is stiff and glossy; this should take no longer than 8 minutes. About 2 minutes before the fluff is ready, add the vanilla.

4   Store the finished fluff in the fridge in an airtight container for up to 2 weeks.

Vegan Fluffed Marshmallow

(Ta to Goose Wohlt)

Goose Wohlt is a vegan food blogger who discovered that the water in tinned chickpeas (known as aquafaba) can be used as an egg white substitute. I have followed his lead to create this marshmallow fluff.

Makes 1 large jam jar
(about 200g)

- 150g granulated sugar
- 400g can of chickpeas
- ¼ tsp cream of tartar
- 1 tsp vanilla extract

1   Pour the sugar into a medium-sized pan and add 50ml of cold water. Bring to a gentle boil, stirring occasionally, until the mixture reaches 116°C on a sugar thermometer.

2   Meanwhile, ensure your stand mixer bowl is clean and dry and has no greasy residue (cleaning it with a small dab of white wine vinegar on kitchen paper works perfectly). Open the chickpeas and drain the liquid into the mixer bowl (save the beans for another recipe). Add the cream of tartar and the vanilla and whip until stiff, about 4 minutes.

3   When the syrup has reached 116°C, gently pour it into the mixer bowl, keeping the whisk on a slow speed to avoid painful splashes. Increase the speed slowly and whip for 15–20 minutes until stiff, glossy and marshmallowy. This will take a while, but have faith.

4   Use as a replacement in all the fluff recipes in this book. Store in the fridge for up to 2 days in an airtight container. If it separates, simply re-beat and it will come back together.

Sweet Shortcrust Pastry

This creates a delicate pastry which provides the perfect base for *tartes* and sweet pies. A lot of recipes use more butter than I have recommended here - but I find this makes the pastry too greasy and less delicate. Always use ice-cold water when making this pastry as it adds a slight elasticity to the dough - making it easier to roll.

Makes 500g

- 150g unsalted butter
- 50g icing sugar, sifted
- 2 medium egg yolks, at room temperature
- ½ tsp sea salt flakes
- ½ tsp vanilla bean paste
- 15ml ice-cold water
- 250g plain flour

1   Place the butter in the bowl of a stand mixer and use the paddle attachment to mix until creamy, scraping down the edges as needed. Add the icing sugar and mix.
2   Now add the egg yolks, sea salt and vanilla with 15ml of very cold water and mix. Add the flour in 3 batches, mixing between each addition. Stop mixing as soon as it starts to form into a dough ball.
3   Cut the dough in half. Wrap half in cling film and let it settle in the fridge for 30 minutes before using. Place the other half in a freezer bag and store in the freezer for another time.

Spring, Paris & Patisserie

As the blossom appeared on the cherry trees lining the boulevards and grand public gardens of Paris, I regularly spent warmer days wandering from pavement cafés to boutiques at an unhurried pace. Crunching on a baguette lined thickly with butter and crammed with freshly sliced ham, I made my way to sugar-induced seduction in the 6th *arrondissement*, home to my favourite chocolatiers. Oh, the *chocolateries*. With their acrylic display cases in neon colours suspended from ceilings, moody nightclub lighting, marble floors that made your shoes squeak and jewel-coloured macarons, pâtes de fruits and painted ganaches: Mind. Blown. On those days of dawdling, contemplating precision-perfect rows of truffles, I found tiny gem-sized *carrés* (squares) of chocolate, carefully stencilled with the origin of their cocoa bean, such as 'Ghana', 'Brazil', and 'Venezuela'. This journey through the world of chocolate came wrapped in layers of glossy black tissue, encased in heavy black boxes (the sort that 'shoosh' when you prise off the lid), tied up with a flourish of silk ribbon. Sold.

My training in Paris was definitely not at this rarefied level. Nor was I welcomed into a twinkling *chocolaterie* by a rosy-cheeked proprietor. Nope. The Ecole Médéric was more like Grange Hill with profiteroles. In France, in order to work as a pastry chef in a professional kitchen, you have to complete the CAP course (Certificat d'Aptitude Professionelle). So that's where I was: in a college class of young Parisians who wanted to go into the kitchens of fancy hotels, or travel the globe, secure that they had been trained in the best city in the world.

The course worked in three-week cycles: I would be in college for one week with other students, all of us learning our ABCroissants. The following two weeks were spent on the job in professional kitchens; we were all given different work placements and mine was at a large events venue, Pavillon Dauphine, on the western outskirts of Paris. It is one of those grand spaces that hosts large weddings at the weekends and dry legal conferences during the working week.

Being one of only 2 girls (in a kitchen of 65 chefs) as well as the only English person, I learned 2 pretty important lessons in my first week there: 1) never leave your spoons unattended when your fellow chefs have access to hot ovens and 2) focus on the worst swear words. The second lesson was learned very quickly after the first.

The Pavillon Dauphine was a long 40-minute scooter ride from where I lived and I arrived, bleary-eyed, at 5.30am. Unless I was on the croissant shift, of course, when the working day started at a punishing 3.30am. Urgh, croissant days were not good days. Down a long gravel path was the service kitchen, all of us with our separate work stations, where we set about making the patisserie for that day's events: 200 small fruit tarts for morning receptions, or vast croque-en-bouche towers for evenings.

Riding my scooter home, with boxes filled with uneaten tarts and gateaux slices

'*Deux mains, deux mains!*' Having never worked in a kitchen before, I was shocked at how inept I was at using both hands to complete any culinary task. Saying it now, it seems quite obvious, but next time you are in the kitchen, perhaps placing bun cases in a baking tray or flouring a surface to roll pastry, just note how little you actually use both hands. Sure, you start with good two-handed intentions… then slowly one drifts down towards your side, swinging aimlessly. If this happens when you work in a pastry kitchen you soon know about it. '*Deux mains, deux mains!*': when that has been screamed into your ear 76 times in a day, that hand stops wandering off so often and you realise you are now a far more efficient chef.

Riding my scooter home, with boxes filled with uneaten tarts and gateau slices, I would race against the early evening Parisian traffic, a swirl of buses, blaring horns and indifferent pedestrians, heading towards the steamy glow of *le centre ville*. Scootering towards the Marais after a day in the kitchen is one of the things I miss the most about being in that city. I didn't know much about the Marais district before arriving in Paris, but within the first month I discovered its *fripes* (or *friperies*) shops: the second-hand clothes shops where vintage denim gems are piled on top of classic Breton tops and antique furs, all costing between €5 and €10.

It seemed as if each small cobbled street of the Marais contained its own style of *fripes* shop, ranging from the fusty, dimly lit stores where you had to climb a ladder to reach the 'good' boxes at the top, to the fluo-strip stalls in former mini supermarkets where the stock was wheeled in on rails and the store changed owner from one week to the next. It was around this district that I made some of my closest friends. We would gather for happy-hour margaritas behind the painted windows of Mexican bars, or carafes of *vin de table* under low lighting and noisy ceiling fans. Opposite was my favourite book shop, which in the evening would be so chock-full of people drinking wine and gossiping that you could easily mistake it for one of the many other bars on the street... until you spilled wine on a book (don't do that, they do *not* like it in there) and snuck out the door.

None of us had enough money to enjoy the food we wanted to eat in restaurants, so midway through our second round of drinks, our dining destination would be decided by whose apartment contained the most promising ingredients, or had enough chairs to bunch around a rickety table. Apartments were always at the top of winding staircases and space was invariably tight, but I never had a bad meal. The kitchen in my flat was kitted out with equipment you would ordinarily find on camping holidays. Camping holidays in the 1970s. Whistle kettles that boiled on top of single-plate stoves that balanced on fold-down work surfaces... that sort of thing. I had no choice but to improvise with dishes and utensils, while the lack of space dictated absolute precision and fastidiousness: something that came in useful when training as a pastry chef.

Apartments were always at the top of winding staircases and space was invariably tight, but I never had a bad meal

Spring Marshmallow Recipes

1

Strawberry & Basil

To infuse a strawberry purée *(see page 14)* with the warm, grassy notes of basil, simply add 3 fresh basil leaves to 200ml strawberry purée in a saucepan and warm through over a low heat. Leave to cool for 30 minutes. Discard the basil leaves and use the purée in the Whole Fruit Marshmallow recipe *(see page 15)*.

2

Vanilla Bean

Replace the fruit purée in the Whole Fruit Marshmallow recipe *(see page 15)* with 190ml of water. Add 1 tsp vanilla bean paste to the stand mixer along with the water and glucose.

4

Lemon & Poppy Seed

Replace the fruit purée in the Whole Fruit Marshmallow recipe *(see page 15)* with the finely grated zest of 1 unwaxed lemon, 90ml freshly squeezed lemon juice and 100ml of water. Once the marshmallow mix has been poured into the tin, scatter generously with poppy seeds.

3

Elderflower

Replace the fruit purée in the Whole Fruit Marshmallow recipe *(see page 15)* with 190ml elderflower pressé, or elderflower liqueur (St Germain).

5

Matcha Green Tea

Spoon 1 tbsp matcha green tea powder into 190ml of freshly boiled water and combine thoroughly. Replace the fruit purée in the Whole Fruit Marshmallow recipe *(see page 15)* with the tea. Optional topping: scatter black sesame seeds over the freshly poured marshmallow mix to add a slightly nutty flavour that complements it perfectly.

Apple Tarte Tatin with Vanilla Bean Fluffed Marshmallow

Serves 8

I learned this classic tart recipe in Paris. Let me debunk a myth about French patisserie: it is not difficult. It just requires time and conscientiousness. Like learning your irregular verbs. There are no short cuts, no vaguely guessing how much of what to put in and when. You just need to set aside some time and do it properly. Well done, A+, go to the top of the class...

- plain flour, to dust
- 250g Sweet Shortcrust Pastry (*see page 20*)
- 5 medium apples (a mix of Cox and Granny Smith is ideal)
- 200g granulated sugar
- 40g unsalted butter
- ½ tsp coarse sea salt
- ½ tsp freshly ground black pepper
- ½ quantity Fluffed Marshmallow (*see page 18*)

1   Find a medium-sized ovenproof frying pan. Flour a work surface and roll out the pastry into a circle about 5mm thick; large enough to hang loosely over the frying pan you've chosen, so use that as a rough template. Rest the rolled-out pastry in the fridge.

2   Peel the apples, remove all the seeds and core and finely slice them.

3   Pour 3 tbsp of water into the ovenproof frying pan and add the sugar. Cook over a medium heat until a light golden brown; avoid overcooking the caramel, as the flavour can dominate the dish.

4   Remove the pan from the heat, and with *great* care (seriously, this caramel stuff is hot) stir in the butter, salt and black pepper until fully mixed. Arrange the apple slices in circles inside the pan. You want to cram as many apples in as you can, so you might have to switch up your circles. Return to a low heat for a further 5–7 minutes, then remove from the heat and allow to cool for 15 minutes. Preheat the oven to 190°C/gas 5.

5   Remove the pastry from the fridge and place it delicately over the top of the pan, pushing it down lightly over the apples at the rim. Bake in the hot oven for 25–30 minutes, or until the pastry is golden on top and the caramel is kind of gooey and dark around the edges.

6   Allow the tart to cool for 5 minutes. Grab a plate (anything larger than the pan) and place it over the top. Please wear oven gloves for this bit! Holding both pan and plate together, flip the pan upside down to release the tart. Serve immediately, with a good dollop of marshmallow fluff.

Lemon & Basil Tart with Elderflower Fluffed Marshmallow

Serves 6–8

Adding peppery basil to lemon gives this tart a very 'grown-up' taste. Eat this instead of getting a mortgage, washing the car or eating all your vegetables.

For the tart

- 150ml double cream
- 3 basil leaves
- 2 tbsp grated unwaxed lemon zest, plus juice of 3 lemons (200ml)
- 5 medium eggs
- 145g caster sugar
- 35ml elderflower pressé
- 250g Sweet Shortcrust Pastry (*see page 20*), chilled
- plain flour, to dust
- edible violets, to serve (optional)

1 To make the filling, heat the cream, basil and lemon zest in a saucepan over a low heat until simmering, to gently infuse the cream. Meanwhile, crack the eggs into a bowl, add the sugar and whisk.

2 When the cream is just below boiling point (80°C), discard the basil, pour the cream into the egg and sugar mix and whisk to combine. When the mixture has cooled, stir in the lemon juice and elderflower pressé. The mix will be glossy and smooth.

3 Preheat the oven to 160°C/gas 3. Remove the pastry from the fridge and roll out on a lightly floured work surface until about the thickness of a £1 coin. Line a round 23cm tart tin with the pastry and push down gently so it fits perfectly. Trim off any excess and prick the bottom with a fork, then chill for 10 minutes to relax the dough.

4 Cover the pastry with baking parchment, fill with baking beans, and blind bake in the hot oven for 15 minutes. Remove the baking beans and paper and bake for a further 15 minutes until the pastry turns a golden biscuit colour. Pour the lemon and elderflower filling into the base and cook for a further 15–20 minutes, until there is only a slight wobble when the filling is touched. Remove the tart from the oven and leave to cool in the tin.

For the fluffed marshmallow

- 1 quantity Fluffed Marshmallow (*see page 18*)
- 80ml elderflower pressé

5 To make the elderflower fluffed marshmallow, replace the water in the recipe (*see page 18*) with 80ml elderflower pressé.

6 Using a piping bag with a round nozzle, pipe on individual kisses of marshmallow fluff to decorate. Alternatively, serve a large dollop of fluff alongside your tart.

Coffee Fluffed Marshmallow Charlotte

Serves 6

I'm pretty greedy... not a glutton, but definitely greedy. I like trying things, especially other people's things. If we aren't already sharing something to eat, then I will lean over to try and nab a bite or steal a sip of whatever you have. Were we to eat a meal together, if you ever had to leave the room, you'd better pay close attention to the contents of your plate before exiting.

This is for those of you with a similar disposition. Whipping up this indulgent layered dessert means you can pop it in the middle of the table and give everyone a spoon to dig in with. You get to eat from the same dish as your dinner companions and things wont get awkward. Yeah, you're welcome.

- 150ml espresso coffee, freshly made, but cooled
- 250ml dark rum
- 400g sponge fingers
- 1 quantity Fluffed Marshmallow (*see page 18*)
- 100g mascarpone cheese
- 1 tsp vanilla bean paste
- cocoa powder, to dust

1   Set out a 20cm square dish; a glass or clear plastic dish will show off the layers nicely, but is not essential. In a shallow bowl, mix the coffee and the rum. Dunk in the sponge fingers, letting them soak up the liquid until damp, not soggy. Use a quarter of the biscuits to line the base of your dish.

2   Make the fluffed marshmallow and place it in a bowl. Mix together the mascarpone and vanilla, then, with a metal spoon, fold this into the fluff in the bowl to give a lighter, moussey consistency.

3   Spoon a quarter of the mascarpone fluff over the biscuit layer and sprinkle lightly with cocoa. Lay half the remaining soaked biscuits on top, then cover with half the remaining mascarpone fluff and sprinkle with cocoa. Repeat the process for the final layer.

4   Cover with cling film and refrigerate overnight. Dust with more cocoa just before serving.

Lemon & Chamomile Madeleines, Fluffed Marshmallow

Makes 24

Any freshly baked sponge is an absolute pleasure to eat but these, being little and French, are as sophisticated as wearing ballet pumps, a Breton top and having bobbed hair. They knock the silly old fairy cake into a shell-shaped tin... literally. If you don't have 2 madeleine tins, just use 1 and bake in 2 batches. The feather-light texture makes them ideal for dipping in hot chocolate or coating in fluffed marshmallow.

Brown butter, which is commonly used in French baking, adds a lovely fragrant, nutty element to this recipe. To make the brown butter, simply melt the butter in a small saucepan over a low heat until it has turned a beautiful deep amber colour. Be careful to remove it from the heat before it burns, as it can quickly catch and turn bitter.

For the madeleines

Equipment: 2 x 12 -hole madeleine trays

○ 75g unsalted butter, melted and browned (see recipe introduction), plus more for the trays
○ 100g plain flour, plus more to dust
○ 2 large eggs
○ pinch of fine salt
○ 75g caster sugar
○ ½ tsp baking powder

1   Butter your madeleine trays and sift over a small handful of flour. Turn over the trays and tip out any excess, then place them in the fridge until you're ready to use them.

2   Crack the eggs into the bowl of a stand mixer, add the salt, and beat on a high speed until the mixture is bubbly and a light yellow colour. Reduce the mixer speed to medium and slowly pour in the sugar. Continue to beat for about 7 minutes, until the mixture has thickened and is a very pale creamy colour.

3   Sift together the flour and baking powder. Remove the bowl from the mixer and spoon in the sifted flour very, very gently, using a rubber spatula to carefully fold it into the egg mixture after each addition of flour. Once all the flour has been fully incorporated, pour in the melted brown butter and carefully fold that in, too.

4   Remove the trays from the fridge and pour 1 heaped tbsp of the mixture into each madeleine mould, then return the trays to the fridge to chill for 1 hour. The resulting thermal reaction when you bake the madeleines will result in the characteristic little nub of this classic cake.

Matcha Green Tea Marshmallow Eclairs

Makes 18

The delicate consistency of eclairs lends itself to more playful flavours. You can adapt this to include any of your favourite marshmallows as a filling. I'm ashamed to admit that I chose matcha for its vibrancy of colour and intensity of taste, not for its antioxidant qualities... although it has lots of those as well.

The high moisture content in choux pastry allows it to rise in the oven resulting in an incredibly light and airy shell. Bake at a high heat for 20 minutes before reducing the temperature and baking until the pastry is crisp and completely and utterly dry.

For the matcha marshmallow cream

∘ 200g good-quality white chocolate
∘ 125g Matcha Green Tea Marshmallows (*see page 27*), chopped
∘ 325ml double cream
∘ ½ tsp matcha green tea powder

1   To make the marshmallow cream, melt the white chocolate using a bain-marie (*see page 10*). Put the chopped marshmallows in a pan over very low heat and stir in the melted white chocolate and 50ml of the cream. Once the mallows are fully melted, add the matcha green tea powder and remove from the heat.
2   In a stand mixer, whisk the remaining cream to soft peaks. Fold the whipped cream slowly into the marshmallow mix, retaining as much air as you can. Leave to cool in the fridge before using.

For the choux pastry

Equipment: piping bag
10mm plain piping
nozzle, 8mm plain
piping nozzle

○ 50ml whole milk
○ 75ml whole milk
○ 1 tbsp caster sugar
○ pinch of fine salt
○ 50g unsalted butter
○ 125g plain flour

1   Preheat the oven to 200°C/gas 6. In a saucepan, mix together the milk, 150ml of water, the sugar, salt and butter and bring to a boil. Remove the pan from the heat and sift in the flour, then beat very quickly with a spatula until you have a completely even paste.

2   Return the pan to a low heat to remove all the moisture from the dough, so that it forms a ball that easily pulls away from the sides. Transfer to a large bowl and allow to cool for 5 minutes. Add the eggs 1 at a time, using a spatula to incorporate each carefully before you add the next.

3   Line a baking tray and whilst the dough is smooth and still warm, transfer to a piping bag and, using a 10mm piping nozzle, pipe the dough into 10–12cm strips on the tray, leaving a gap of 3cm between each so they have room to expand during baking.

4   Bake for 20 minutes, and then reduce the oven heat to 180°C and bake for a further 15–18 minutes until firm and golden. Do not open the oven door during this process.

5   Remove from the oven and leave to cool on a cooling rack.

6   To fill the eclairs, using an 8mm plain nozzle, poke 3 holes into the underside of each, 1 in the centre and 1 on either side. Transfer the marshmallow cream to a piping bag fitted with the 8mm nozzle and squeeze into the 3 holes. (Or, if you don't own pastry nozzles, cut the eclair in half horizontally using a serrated knife, spoon marshmallow cream on the bottom layer and place the other half on top.)

For the white chocolate fondant

- 150g icing sugar
- 20ml glucose (optional, but it gives a shinier finish)
- 60g good-quality white chocolate
- matcha green tea powder, to decorate
- black sesame seeds, to serve (optional)

1 Sift the icing sugar into a medium-sized saucepan and very gradually stir in 20ml of cold water and the glucose, if using, adding only a very little at a time. When the fondant is completely smooth and falls off the spoon in heavy ribbons (you may need to add a tiny bit more water), place it over a very low heat to warm it through, continuing to stir regularly.

2 In a separate bowl melt the chocolate over a bain-marie *(see page 10)*. Once the chocolate has melted and is of a similar temperature to the fondant, scrape it into the fondant pan and mix thoroughly.

3 Dip the top of each filled eclair into chocolate fondant to coat, and sprinkle lightly with matcha green tea powder and black sesame, if you like. Allow to cool.

Summer, Friends & Outdoor Eating

Being outside in the summer months should be a freckle-splattered riot of long days and hot nights. But summer doesn't like Paris very much. It finds the city too hot, too quiet and too lacking in space. Those wide boulevards become oppressive when all summer wants to do is loll about on the grass. None of the Parisian apartments I lived in were blessed with balconies or simple-to-open windows, so I shared summer's disdain. Easy-going indoor dining, so convivial for ten months of the year, became claustrophobic and far too much – urgh – effort.

We all know that food tastes better when eaten outside, but I also suspect that summer food tastes good because it's motivated by lethargy: a 'that'll do, let's fling it together and just go to the park' lighter touch. A culinary undressing.

My summer days in Paris were spent searching out a spare patch of grass at the Buttes-Chaumont park, or outside the rambling terrace cafés by the Canal Saint-Martin, drinking sticky cola from a glass bottle, fantasising about stowing away on a sleeper train to the beach.

Before spending a fourth summer in Paris I came home. That summer was filled with food festivals, street feasts and outdoor concerts, banquets and bonfires, culminating in London and the blow-out weekend of the year: the Notting Hill Carnival, a vivid street spectacle of vibrant beats, spicy food and exhilarating abandonment, dancing, drinking, jostling, banging and whistling. A frantic few days of doing things you're not normally allowed to do in public. Notting Hill, with its brazen mash-up of foods and cultural twists, was the place I started to prepare traditional French sweets... but with that London edge (think: a slosh of gin and a cup of tea).

Summer Marshmallow Recipes

1
Raspberry & Champagne

My best-selling flavour because, deep down, we all love a bit of posh. I use rosé champagne to give it a light sparkling lift and enhance the berries. You will need 190ml raspberry purée (*see page 14*). Use it to make the Whole Fruit Marshmallow recipe (*see page 15*). Just before the marshmallows are ready to be poured out, add 30ml rosé champagne and continue to whip. The champagne will loosen the mixture, but whisk on high speed for 5 minutes until it comes back up.

2
Passion Fruit & Ginger

Intense passion fruit warmed with a touch of fiery ginger, this is my favourite flavour. I really recommend trying to find passion fruit purée, as it is notoriously difficult to extract the juice. But if you have to: take 9 passion fruits, slice in half and scoop out the insides. Force the pulp through a fine sieve with a spoon. Finely grate in a 2.5cm piece of peeled root ginger, and use in the Whole Fruit Marshmallow recipe (*see page 15*).

3
Mango & Sweet Orange

My Alphonso mango marshmallow accented by a dash of sweet orange is most popular with our younger fans. Replace the 190ml purée used in the Whole Fruit Marshmallow recipe (*see page 15*) with 150ml mango purée mixed with 40ml freshly squeezed orange juice.

4
Raspberry, Rose & Pistachio

Make up the Whole Fruit Marshmallow recipe (*see page 15*) , using 190ml raspberry purée. Just before the end of whipping, pour in 1 tsp good-quality rose water and continue to whip on a high speed. Once the marshmallow has set and been cut into squares, roll them in finely ground pistachio nuts to coat.

Lemon-Ginger Layer Cake with Fluffed Frosting

(A cake for Suzy and Laura)

Serves 10–12

As a child, my annual summer holidays were spent on family camping trips to the south of France. Every year we went to the same Pyrenean site and my brother, sister and I, alongside an ever-expanding band of friends, would run semi-feral for 4 long blissful weeks.

Our very good family friends, the Hollands, would always be there with us, and 2 of their daughters' birthdays fell during these holiday weeks. Each was celebrated with a makeshift tea party, of sorts. No birthday was ever allowed to pass without some fundamental ingredients: Carambars caramel candy, Prince chocolate biscuits, odd little crackers that tasted of pizza and the Paul Simon *Graceland* album on cassette. The pièce de résistance of the party (and subsequent butt of many family jokes) was the 'cake'. Children were hushed, candles were lit and the it was carried to the table. Then, following a rousing chorus of 'Happy Birthday', presented to the birthday girl would be… a pear flan.

A pear flan? No child *ever* wants that for their birthday. Not now, and not in 1994. But birthday cakes were not to be found in rural French *supermarchés* and, besides, we were pretty sick from all those Carambars anyway. The parents, however, thoroughly enjoyed pear flan… hmm, I bet they did.

So this light lemon cake with a cheeky hit of spice and a celebratory frosting is dedicated to Suzy and Laura Holland, to make up for all those pear flans. *Bon anniversaire*!

For the lemon curd (optional)

Makes 2 large 180g jam jars (or you can use shop-bought curd)

○ grated zest and juice of 6 unwaxed lemons
○ 300g caster sugar
○ 200g unsalted butter, cut into cubes
○ 5 medium eggs, plus 1 egg yolk

1   If you are making your own curd, do so first. Put the lemon zest and juice, sugar and butter into a heatproof bowl and heat over a bain-marie *(see page 10)*. Whisk the mixture from time to time until the butter has completely melted and the sugar has fully dissolved.

2   In a separate bowl, lightly whisk the eggs and egg yolk together, then stir into the lemon mixture. Let the curd cook in the bain-marie, stirring regularly, for about 10 minutes, until it is thick and creamy and coats the back of a spoon.

3   Remove from the heat and pour into 2 hot sterilised jars*. When cool, the curd will keep for up to 2 weeks in the fridge.

For the cake

○ 350g unsalted butter, softened, plus more for the tins
○ 450g caster sugar
○ 6 large eggs, lightly beaten
○ 30ml good-quality olive oil
○ 450g self-raising flour
○ 3 tbsp lemon curd
○ grated zest of 2 lemons

4   Preheat the oven to 180°C/gas 4. Lightly butter 2 × 20cm loose-based sandwich tins and line with baking parchment.

5   Cream together the butter and caster sugar in a stand mixer on medium speed until pale, light and fluffy. In a separate bowl, lightly beat the eggs and oil together, then very gradually add this to the mixer bowl, mixing well on a medium speed between each addition.

6   Sift the flour into the mixture and mix on a low speed to combine. Add the lemon curd and mix until smooth.

7   Pour the mixture into the prepared cake tins and smooth the surfaces with a palette knife. Bake in the hot oven for 45–50 minutes, until well risen and a skewer inserted into the middles comes out clean. It's important to keep your eye on the cakes during baking; if they start to become too dark before being fully cooked, cover with foil to finish. Remove from the oven.

For the lemon-ginger syrup

- juice of 1 lemon
- small knob of root ginger, cut into thin rounds
- 8 tbsp granulated sugar

8   Meanwhile, place the lemon juice in a small pan, add the ginger, sugar and 75ml of water and warm through over a low heat until the sugar has fully dissolved.

9   Slowly spoon the syrup over the top of the warm cakes to moisten. Leave the cakes to cool completely in the tins, before removing from the tins and placing on a cooling rack. Once the cakes are cold, cut each in half horizontally using a long serrated bread knife, making 4 layers in total.

For the filling and frosting

- 1 jar lemon curd
- 1 quantity Fluffed Marshmallow (*see page 18*)
- candles, to finish

10   Place a first layer of cake cut side up on a plate, spoon 3 large tbsp of lemon curd on and spread out, then place a second layer of cake on top, again cut side up. Spoon 2 large spoonfuls of fluffed mallow on top; leave a good 2cm rim round the edge as the fluff smooshes out when you place more layers on top. Cover with a third layer of cake, cut side up, top with more lemon curd and then the final layer of cake, this time cut side down, so you have the most even layer on top. Using a palette knife, apply fluffed mallow all over the top and sides.

11   With a mini blowtorch, torch the outside of the cake to give a delicate toasted crunch and top with, of course, candles..

*To sterilise jars: heat the oven to 180°C/gas 4, place the clean jars on an oven tray – do not let the jars touch! – and heat for at least 20 minutes. Place their lids in a bowl and cover with boiling water from the kettle. Dry with kitchen paper and use while both jars and their prospective contents are still warm.

Persian Raspberry, Rose & Pistachio Cake

(A love cake)

Serves 8

Once upon a time, in a fruit punnet not far from here, was a Raspberry. This Raspberry was, to be frank, a little fed up with its lot in life. Please don't ask me why. One morning, when the Raspberry was sat sullenly minding its own business, a delicate waft of floral musk drifted by. The Raspberry's head was well and truly turned. Quite unexpectedly, Rose had entered its life. Things were looking up. The Rose, fully aware that it could be a bit much – a touch sickly and a tad sweet – was tamed by the sourness of Raspberry and, in turn, Raspberry flourished under Rose's heady exoticism.

I'm not going to tell you how they got all mixed up with pistachios... that's best left to the imagination.

For the cake

- 60ml vegetable oil, plus more for the tin
- 140g plain flour
- pinch of fine salt
- 60g caster sugar
- 9g baking powder
- 3 medium eggs, separated
- 1 tsp grated unwaxed lemon zest

1   Preheat the oven to 180°C/gas 4. Line the base of 2 × 15cm round cake tins with baking parchment and oil the sides.

2   Mix all the dry ingredients together: flour, salt, sugar and baking powder. In a separate bowl, whisk the egg yolks with 80ml of water and the oil until doubled in size and fluffy, then add the lemon zest. Mix this into the dry mixture to make a thick batter.

3   Whisk the egg whites until stiff, then fold very gently into the batter; you want a very light sponge cake, so retaining as much air as possible from the whisked egg whites is essential.

4   Divide the batter equally between the prepared cake tins and bake in the hot oven for 20 minutes, or until a skewer inserted into the middles comes out clean. Leave to cool completely on a rack.

For the rose fluffed marshmallow

- 1 quantity Fluffed Marshmallow (*see page 18*)
- 1 tsp good-quality rose water

5 To make the rose fluffed marshmallow, follow the recipe for Fluffed Marshmallow (*see page 18*), replacing the vanilla bean paste with the rose water.

To decorate

- 1 punnet of raspberries
- 4 handfuls of unsalted pistachio nuts, shelled
- 1 handful of dried edible rose petals

6 Once your cakes have cooled, slice each cake in half, horizontally, with a serrated knife.

7 Spread the rose fluffed mallow on the top of one of your cake halves, and scatter a handful of raspberries and pistachios on top. This is your bottom layer.

8 Add a second layer on top of the mallow, and cover the top of it with fluffed mallow, raspberries and pistachios again. Repeat for the third and fourth layers, finishing the fourth with rose petals as well as raspberries and pistachios.

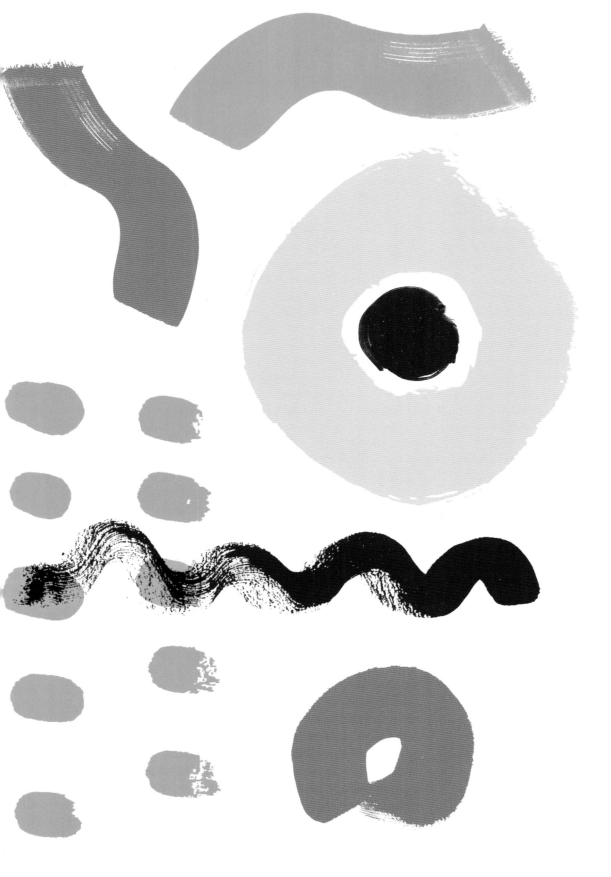

Raspberry & Champagne Ice Pops

Serves 6

What's cooler than being cool? My Raspberry & Champagne Ice Pops, that's what. Using the flavour pairing from my best-selling marshmallow these ice pops are even easier to make than to nipping to the corner shop. A bit classier too. You can make them into whatever shape pop moulds you prefer but though it might be tempting.. It might be incredibly tempting to slosh a bit more booze into these, but remember, alcohol does not freeze (unless slightly watered down), so try to stick to this recipe as best you can.

Equipment: 6 ice pop moulds, plus sticks

○ 250g granulated sugar *(to make Basic Sugar Syrup)*
○ 70ml raspberry Fruit Purée *(see page 14)*
○ 150ml champagne (or cava or prosecco work just as well and are a bit less spendy)
○ 90ml cold water

1 First, make your sugar syrup. Boil up the sugar and 250ml of water in a pan until the sugar has fully dissolved, then leave to cool. You only need 30ml for this recipe, but it is useful stuff and keeps for a couple of weeks in the fridge.

2 Measure out 30 ml of sugar syrup, then mix with all the ingredients together into a measuring jug with 70ml of cold water.

2 Pour evenly into 6 ice pop moulds. Be careful not to fill them to the top, so as to allow for expansion in the freezer.

3 Insert the pop sticks and freeze overnight.

Toasted Marshmallow Ice Cream

Serves 4

Yup, toasted marshmallow ice cream. All the very best bits of summer, from campfires to beaches, churned into each indulgent lick. I use an ice cream maker for this, but it is just as easy to make by hand.

- 10 × 4.5cm square marshmallows, any flavour *(see page 14)*
- a little flavourless vegetable oil
- 250ml whole milk
- 5 large egg yolks
- 100g golden caster sugar
- ¼ tsp salt
- 700ml double cream
- 2 large handfuls of ice cubes

1   Line a baking tray with baking parchment, and preheat the grill to medium-high. Set the marshmallows on the prepared tray and pop under the grill. When they are all slightly browned on one side, turn them over with an oiled spatula to toast on the other side. Set aside.

2   Using a medium-sized pan, heat the milk until it starts to simmer. Meanwhile, in a large bowl, whisk together the egg yolks, sugar and salt. When the milk starts to simmer, take the pan off the heat and pour half the hot milk into the egg yolk mixture, whisking vigorously until fully incorporated. Whisk all the egg yolk mixture into the hot milk in the saucepan.

3   Cook over a low heat for 6–8 minutes, stirring continuously with a wooden spoon to ensure that the eggs don't curdle. The custard is ready when it is thick enough to hold a finger-drawn line across the back of the wooden spoon without dripping.

4   Remove the pan from the heat and mix in the cream and toasted marshmallows.* For making ice cream, it's really important to cool the custard as quickly as possible, so transfer it to a cold bowl sat in a larger bowl filled with water and ice cubes and stir occasionally until cool. Once cool, strain the custard into a sealable container and place in the fridge overnight (it will keep for a couple of days).

5   Pour the ice cream mix into an ice cream maker and, once churned, cover and freeze for 1 hour before serving. Or, to make the ice cream by hand, stir it well with a fork and place in the freezer for 1 hour. Remove and beat with a fork until uniform in consistency. Repeat 3 times, then freeze, covered, for 1 hour before serving.

* At this stage, the custard can be poured into a jug and used as a delicious topping for my Rhubarb & Rosemary Rumble *(see page 102)*.

Passion Fruit & Yuzu Cheesecake

Serves 6–8

Pairing refreshing passion fruits with just a touch of the face-puckeringly sour citrus juice of Japanese yuzu fruit gives this super-creamy cheesecake a satisfying tang.

- 200g good-quality ginger nut biscuits
- 100g unsalted butter, plus more for the tin
- 600g mascarpone
- 150g cream cheese
- 150ml double cream
- 75g icing sugar
- 1 tsp yuzu juice
- 100g Passion Fruit & Ginger Marshmallows *(see page 51)*, chopped
- 10g pre-soaked gelatine leaves *(see page 11)*
- 2 passion fruits, to decorate

1   To make the ginger nut base, place the biscuits in a ziplock bag and bash with a rolling pin to a very coarse crumb. Melt the butter over a low heat and mix into the biscuit crumbs. Lightly butter a 25cm loose-bottomed cake tin and press the crumbs into the base and slightly up the sides. Leave in the fridge to chill for 30 minutes.

2   To make the filling, beat together the mascarpone and cream cheese in a bowl until smooth, then set aside. In a saucepan over a low heat, mix together the double cream, icing sugar, yuzu juice and marshmallows. Heat through until fully melted and combined.

3   Remove from the heat and add the soaked gelatine. Return the pan to a low heat and stir constantly, until the gelatine has completely melted. Take off the heat and allow to cool for 5 minutes.

4   Fold the creamy marshmallow mix into the mascarpone mix and combine thoroughly; the consistency should be thick and mousse-like in texture. Pour on to the base and pop in the fridge to set for 4 hours.

5   Carefully remove the cheesecake from the tin (if it's slightly stuck, running a warm knife around the edge will help). Spoon out the flesh of the passion fruits and scatter it evenly on top.

Raspberry Marshmallow & Macadamia Blondie

Makes 10

The blondie – the Debbie Harry to Chrissie Hynde's brownie – lighter on top but with the same tight leather trousers and uncompromising stare; a statuesque grande dame of the dessert world, as satisfying as that laconic rap in *Rapture* and a smudgy rim of eyeliner. I use raspberry and champagne marsh-mallows to further lighten the texture, my culinary equivalent of peroxide.

- 125g unsalted butter, plus more for the tin
- 180g best-quality white chocolate, chopped
- 4 medium eggs
- 150g golden caster sugar
- 200g white caster sugar
- 250g plain flour
- ¼ tsp baking powder
- pinch of seasalt flakes
- 150g Raspberry & Champagne Marshmallows, chopped *(see page 51)*
- 100g toasted macadamia nuts, roughly chopped
- 50g pistachio nuts, roughly chopped

1   Preheat the oven to 180°C/gas 4. Line a 20cm square cake tin with greaseproof paper and butter it well. Melt the butter in a small heavy-based saucepan and cook over a low heat to make brown butter *(see page 38)*. Once it has reached the perfect amber colour, remove the pan from the heat, add the chocolate pieces and melt slowly, stirring occasionally, before leaving to cool for 5 minutes.

2   Meanwhile, beat the eggs and both sugars together in a stand mixer (or with a hand-held whisk) until pale and mousse-like in texture. This will take about 5 minutes.

3   Gently pour the melted chocolate and butter mixture into the sweetened egg mixture and whisk lightly until combined. Sift in the flour, baking powder and salt and fold in gently. Add the raspberry marshmallows and pistachios, and stir until well distributed.

4   Scatter the chopped macadamia nuts over the prepared tin. Scrape the blondie mixture into the tray and smooth out. Bake in the hot oven for 30–35 minutes (depending on how gooey you like your blondies, I recommend checking very frequently at this stage with the tip of a skewer).

5   Remove from the oven and leave in the tin to cool for at least 1 hour. Cut into squares with a sharp knife, then lift them out of the tin.

6   These will keep for 3 days in an airtight container, or can be frozen for up to 1 month.

Squidgy Granola Bars

Makes 10–12

Wrapped in greaseproof paper and tied with string, these make for a great pick-me-up at festivals, in the park or on picnics. You can use any berries or combinations of nuts-seeds-fruits you like, or have in the cupboard.

Sometimes I like to drizzle these bars with melted white chocolate, for an extra chocolate boost. If you want to do the same, you will need about 100g white chocolate.

- unsalted butter, for the tin
- 370g rolled oats
- 100g dried cranberries, coarsely chopped
- 100g shelled salted pistachios, chopped
- 100g shredded sweetened coconut, chopped
- 300g good-quality dark chocolate, roughly chopped
- 3 tbsp runny honey
- 200g marshmallows (any flavour you like), chopped

1   Preheat the oven to 170°C/gas 3 and lightly butter a 20cm square baking tin.

2   Spread the oats evenly over a large baking tray and pop in the oven for 8–10 minutes until lightly browned, stirring halfway through so they brown evenly.

3   Place the toasted oats in a large bowl and add the cranberries, pistachios, coconut and dark chocolate; set aside. In a small pan over medium heat, combine the honey and marshmallows and melt down over a gentle heat, stirring continuously. Stir the melted mixture into the bowl of dry ingredients and mix thoroughly.

4   Press the mixture into the prepared tin and bake for 13 minutes. Allow to cool completely in the tin, then remove and cut into bars.

BBQ Pineapple with Rum Fluffed Marshmallow

Serves 6

Outdoor fires at anytime of the year are special –peaty smoke that hugs your clothes, flames that leak a bit further out than feels entirely safe and that cheeky little crackle of the wood- but especially in the summer. Summer grills, bonfires and BBQs are not often associated with desserts but using embers to scorch or toast fruit gives an intensity of flavour that is hard to recreate in the kitchen.

This recipe is so syrupy and gorgeous, you will want to chase it down the street and give it a bear hug. Don't. It's too sticky. Just eat it properly, like a normal person.

For the rum fluffed marshmallow

○ Fluffed Marshmallow
(see page 18)
○ 80ml spiced dark rum

1   To make the rum fluffed marshmallow, follow the recipe for Fluffed Marshmallow *(see page 18),* replacing the vanilla bean paste with the spiced dark rum.

For the BBQ pineapple

○ 1 ripe pineapple, peeled and sliced into 6 even rounds
○ 200g dark muscovado sugar
○ 2 shots of dark spiced rum
○ sweet spice, to taste, such as cinnamon, nutmeg or ginger

2   Preheat the barbecue. Arrange the pineapple slices in a shallow dish and coat liberally with the dark muscovado sugar, rum and a sprinkling of spice. Place in the fridge for about 30 minutes to let the pineapple absorb all the lovely flavours.

3   Arrange the slices on a grate over the barbecue and cook until softened and lightly charred. (Alternatively, if it's a tad too wet to do this outside, preheat your grill to medium-high, set the pineapple slices in a baking tray and grill for 10 minutes.)

4   Once the pineapple slices are soft and caramelised, remove from the fire and put into individual serving bowls. Serve with rum fluffed marshmallow spooned liberally on top. Torch the fluff lightly with a blowtorch to add an extra rich caramelised hit.

S'mores, two ways

Many of my favourite recipes are created when I need to please a crowd. Recently I have found that the best way to round off a late-night gathering is to set up a s'mores 'station' (all right, normally it's just a tabletop or the lid of a cool box, but 'station' sounds better).

Toasting marshmallows turns a treat into an experience. I started providing firepits to toast mallows at summer festivals and couldn't believe how popular it was. Fruit marshmallows don't burn, they melt. The heat draws out the purées so that the flavours are amplified. Also, people just really like fires.

I created this showstopper of a s'more for a dessert at a lavish Indian wedding in Florence. The melted marshmallows and shards of cracked chocolate sandwiched between fine crisp biscuits with a honey laced ganache binding the mallow and chocolate shards together was a huge hit and kept the guests dancing until the small hours.

To create your s'mores, first chop your chocolate (white, milk or dark) into shards. Place a teaspoon of honey ganache (see over the page) onto a thin biscuit: choose either the ginger snaps below or the lemon shortbread over the page, sprinkle on a tiny pinch of salt, smooch a toasted marshmallow over the ganache before placing a shard of chocolate on top and sandwiching it all with a final biscuit.

For the ginger snap biscuits

Makes 24

- 115g unsalted butter
- 120g dark muscovado sugar
- 150ml molasses
- 300g plain flour, plus more to dust
- 1 tsp bicarbonate of soda
- 2 tsp ground ginger
- 2 tsp allspice
- grated zest of ½ orange

1   Preheat the oven to 190°C/gas 5. Line a baking sheet with baking parchment.
2   Place the butter, sugar and molasses in a large saucepan over a medium heat. Stir until smooth and beginning to simmer.
3   Remove the pan from the heat and sift in the flour, bicarbonate of soda and spices. Stir in the orange zest and mix with a spatula until it forms a dough. Leave to cool for 30 minutes.
4   Turn out the dough on to a lightly floured work surface and roll out to 2cm thick. Cut into 5cm squares, you should get 24 biscuits. Place the biscuits on the prepared baking tray and bake in the hot oven until crisp, 8–10 minutes. Let cool on the baking tray before transferring to a cooling rack with a palette knife to cool completely.

It can be easy to feel overwhelmed by the bustle of Portobello Road in full mid-morning swing; you could probably stand stock still yet be carried along the street by the relentless throb of tourists. Before they arrive, though, there is a different sort of bustle: a soothing hum of pavements being brushed down; a rustle of tarpaulins as they are lifted from trestle tables; meticulous merchandising of products ranging from antique plates to fedora hats and vintage maps. A whole street of curiosity shops pops up before I've finished my first cup of tea.

I always wanted my pitch to feel unexpected for a marshmallow stall: nothing too soft or pastel or kitsch. The flavours had an edge, so why shouldn't the displays? I used brown greaseproof paper and black electrical tape alongside reclaimed wood and copper piping. The marshmallows, cut into their perfect squidgy cubes, oozing with their soft fruit flavourings, contrasted charmingly.

Just one more cup of tea and I was open for business.

Music seeps out from every space on that street, you only notice it so much when you spend the whole day in the same spot. The pubs with lazy afternoon gigs, or the ambient moods from the newer chain bars, almost drowning out the busker rhythmically thumping his double bass on the crossroads and, my favourite, the floppy-haired guitarist who every Saturday performs such a rousing version of U2's 'I Still Haven't Found What I'm Looking For' that passers-by can't help but join in with him. You would think it would get wearisome, but it doesn't.

A whole street of curiosity shops pops up before I've finished my first cup of tea

Before the lunchtime crowds hit me, I spend a good hour playing the 'if you could have anything *in the world* to eat right now...' game (pretty self-explanatory, but a lot of fun when it is barely more than a couple of minutes' walk between you and your chosen delicacy). Will it be the juicy chicken burger from 'the German Stall' – this may have a different proper name for all that I know, but I have never heard it called anything other than just 'the German Stall' – with its crisp charred skin hot from the griddle, a pokey chilli salsa and a slice of runny American cheese on a white floury bap? Should I go for some light, crisp *churros*, dusted in sugar and cinnamon and with that smell, that hot, sweet, fried smell that I would blindly follow across six lanes of traffic? Then again, maybe I should plump for the flaky sausage rolls with the unctuous fat that drips down your hand, from the deli on Elgin Crescent...

Undoubtedly, autumn is the best season to be on the stall. Winter hunches everyone down into their coat collars; the most attention you'll get is a cursory side-glance as they recce their next access to warmth. Then, in the summer, people melt into pavement corners, flake about on the edge of windowsills or loiter on plastic café furniture. It takes a lorra lorra smiling and hustling to make money on those Saturdays and not just smiling, either: I offer vats of my home-made hot chocolate (*see page 118*) from November through to February, and ice-cold fiery lemonade from June until August.

In those lovely autumn months, the mornings just smell kind of exciting

Shoulders are loose, dawdling is rewarded, the indoors and outdoors seem to rub along a bit better. People come for a chat, buy marshmallows, go for a drink, then come back to buy more to take home or to give to friends.

Autumn Marshmallow Recipes

1
Blueberry & Gin

Vibrant in colour, yet delicate on the palate. I add a nip of Sipsmith London Dry Gin to the batch and highlight its juniper flavour with a small handful of juniper berries, giving a light, almost floral note. Make up ½ quantity Fruit Purée *(see page 14)*, using 200g blueberries and 20g juniper berries, and use in the Whole Fruit Marshmallow recipe *(see page 15)*. About 2 minutes before it is ready to be poured out, add 30ml gin. The gin will loosen the mixture, but whisk on high speed for 5 minutes until it fluffs back up.

2
Campari

Follow the Whole Fruit Marshmallow recipe *(see page 15)*, but replace the fruit purée with 90ml of Campari tipped into the bowl of the stand mixer, along with 100ml of water and the grated zest of ½ orange.

4
Caramelised Apple

Peel, core and halve 3 apples. Sprinkle with brown sugar, cinnamon and nutmeg, lay in a frying pan with a small knob of unsalted butter and cook for 15 minutes. Pour in 1 tbsp rum or orange juice and cook for a further 5 minutes. Use in the Whole Fruit Marshmallow recipe *(see page 15)*.

3
Earl Grey

Make 190ml Earl Grey tea, using 3 tea bags. Follow the Whole Fruit Marshmallow recipe *(see page 15)*, replacing the fruit purée with the tea.

5
Spiced pumpkin

Follow the fruit purée chart *(see page 14)*, and use the pumpkin purée in the Whole Fruit Marshmallow recipe *(see page 15)*, adding a dash of orange juice and ground cinnamon. Save the pumpkin seeds: place them in a bowl of water with their pulp and rub the lot together; the seeds will float free. Dry the seeds, toast them, then crush with cumin seeds and cayenne pepper. Scatter them on the mallows before they are left to set overnight.

Tequila, Lime & Chilli Marshmallows

*Makes 25 full-size
(4.5cm square) marshmallows*

These are my *Dia de los Muertos* marshmallows. They contain almost a whole shot of tequila each – *ay, caramba*! Serve only when expecting the souls of dead relatives.

o ingredients for 1 quantity Whole Fruit Marshmallow *(see page 15)*
o 300ml tequila
o 2 chipotle chillies
o 90ml freshly squeezed lime juice

1   Follow the Whole Fruit Marshmallow recipe *(see page 15)*, but soak the 27g of gelatine in the tequila instead of water. Place the soaked gelatine and tequila in a microwaveable bowl. Heat in the microwave for 1 minute until completely melted.
2   Pour 150ml of water into a small saucepan, add the chipotle chillies and simmer gently over a low heat until just below boiling. Remove from the heat and leave to infuse for 15 minutes.
3   Discard the chillies and use 100ml of the chilli water plus the lime juice instead of the fruit purée in the Whole Fruit Marshmallow recipe. Continue with the recipe as instructed.

Mookies

Makes 12

Ever since the celebrated New York 'Cronut' rocked up to the pastry party, the pressure has been on to create an equally successful hybrid. So hold on to your waistbands, because here it is: the marshmallow-cookie 'Mookie', or as lovely Yorkshire friends and family call it, the 'Mucky' (you have to at least attempt a Yorkshire accent here, please). I'm sure you'll agree it is a far more appropriate name for such a naughty little treat.

○ 150g salted butter, softened
○ 100g light brown muscovado sugar
○ 80g granulated sugar
○ 2 medium eggs
○ 2 tsp vanilla bean paste
○ 250g plain flour, plus more to dust
○ ½ tsp bicarbonate of soda
○ 1 tsp coarse sea salt
○ 200g good-quality dark chocolate, chopped into chunks
○ 100g chopped marshmallows, any flavour, though I'm a fan of Coconut Marshmallows for this (*see page 108*)

1   Place the butter and both sugars into the bowl of a stand mixer and cream together until light and fluffy. Then slowly beat in the eggs 1 at a time and add the vanilla on a medium speed.

2   Remove the bowl from the mixer, gradually sift in the flour, bicarb and salt and fold in carefully with a wooden spoon. Once fully mixed, toss in the chocolate chunks and stir until just combined; try to avoid over-mixing here, or the gluten in the flour develops and your Mookies become hard and tough.

3   Scrape out the mixture on to a floured work surface, divide in half and roll each into a 30cm-long sausage shape. Wrap in cling film and place in the fridge for a minimum of 1 hour to firm up.

4   Preheat the oven to 190°C/gas 5, and line a 44 × 37cm baking tray with baking parchment.

5   Cut each dough sausage into 12 slices, each about 2.5cm wide, to make 24 slices in total, and flatten them down using the palm of your hand. Place a squidge of marshmallow carefully in the centre of one slice, cover with another piece of dough roughly similar in size to the first and press together. Repeat until you've used up all your dough, and place the Mookies on the prepared tray.

6   Bake in the preheated oven for 10–12 minutes, until lightly browned on the edges and soft and mallowy in the centre. Let your Mookies sit in the tray to firm up slightly before transferring to a cooling rack.

Wobbly Road

Makes 14 squares

There is something just lip-smackingly fabulous about trashy American desserts, especially those that don't involve much precision, just a bit of 'chuck-it-all-in' confidence. This version of the classic rocky road is all stone-washed jeans, big-haired, red sports car brashness. Eat while pretending you're Ferris Bueller, on his day off.

- 250g ginger nut biscuits
- 125g unsalted butter, softened
- 300g good-quality dark chocolate, bashed into pieces
- 3 tbsp golden syrup
- 150g marshmallows, chopped; in this recipe I love a mix of Raspberry & Champagne (*see page 51*) and Coconut (*see page 108*)
- optional additions: 50g dried fruits, candied peel, nuts
- icing sugar, to dust

1   Line a 15cm square baking tin with cling film. Place the ginger nut biscuits in a sealable freezer bag and bash with a rolling pin until you have a mixture of large and small crumbs.

2   Melt the butter, chocolate and golden syrup in a bain-marie (*see page 10*), until you have a silky-smooth chocolate sauce. Remove from the heat and fold in the broken biscuits, chopped marshmallows and any extra fruit or nuts, if using.

3   Pour the mixture into the prepared tray and smooth out with a spatula. Store in the fridge overnight.

4   Using a warm, sharp knife, cut the Wobbly Road into squares and dust lightly with icing sugar.

Poached Pears with Caramelised Apple Marshmallow

Serves 4

'Cor blimey, guv'nor, if there's one fing you need frum a Laaandan autumn chapter it's 'ow to make summink aht of all vose Apples and Pears.'

This is a satisfyingly autumnal recipe; the cardamom provides a warming pep. Awwight me ol' china?

○ 6 cardamom pods, cracked open to reveal the seeds
○ 150g granulated sugar
○ 1½ tbsp freshly squeezed lemon juice
○ 4 firm pears, peeled, but stems left on
○ 5 Caramelised Apple Marshmallows
(see page 85)

1 In a large saucepan, stir together the cracked cardamom pods, sugar and lemon juice with 600ml of water and place over a low heat to warm through, stirring occasionally until the sugar has dissolved. Meanwhile, cut the pears in half vertically and remove any seeds.
2 When the sugar has dissolved, increase the heat to a gentle simmer and add the pears to the pan. Cover with a lid and poach until tender; a knife should slide easily through the flesh (25–30 minutes). Remove the pears from the poaching syrup with a slotted spoon and transfer to a serving dish.
3 Boil the poaching liquid until reduced to a thick syrup and stir in the marshmallows until fully melted. Pour the apple mallow syrup over the pears and serve.

Rhubarb & Rosemary Rumble

Serves 6 – 8

The woody, pine-y aroma of rosemary could be thought an unwelcome addition to this pudding but, trust me, it pairs beautifully with the softly stewed rhubarb stalks. Rosemary is surprisingly subtle and even makes the rhubarb a little sweeter, probably by using its eerie herb voodoo. Serve with a shameful amount of toasted marshmallow custard *(see page 66)*.

- 500g rhubarb, chopped into smallish chunks
- 100g golden caster sugar
- 20ml freshly squeezed lemon juice
- 2 sprigs of rosemary
- 180g plain flour
- 110g unsalted butter, cut into cubes and softened
- 110g demerara sugar
- toasted marshmallow custard *(see page 66)*

1 Weigh the rhubarb into a pan and cover with the caster sugar, the lemon juice and the rosemary. Pop on a lid and simmer on a very low heat for 15 minutes. When the rhubarb is soft (but not mushy), discard the rosemary and pour into a 20cm square baking dish. Meanwhile, preheat the oven to 180°C/gas 4.

2 To make the crumble topping, rub together the flour and butter with your fingers until soft, then add the demerara sugar and mix through until it resembles a fine sand.

3 Sprinkle the crumble over the rhubarb and bake in the preheated oven for 30–35 minutes, or until the topping is crisp and golden and the filling is bubbling away underneath. Serve covered with toasted marshmallow custard.

The Cotton Mouth Killer Cocktail

by Trailer Happiness

Makes 1

When I pack up the stall on a Saturday night, my attention turns to one thing: cocktails. I love a good cocktail, and if I've had a few of 'em; I'll even love a bad one. I created the Campari Marshmallow *(see page 85)* for one of the delicious drinks at Trailer Happiness, a tiki lounge on Portobello Road, and now their Cotton Mouth Killer is one of my favourite tipples. So pop on a hula skirt and luau out to this little number.

∘ 20ml lemon juice
∘ 15ml apricot brandy
∘ 60ml strong spiced rum (ideally Sailor Jerry)
∘ 40ml guava juice
∘ 40ml cloudy apple juice
∘ ice cubes
∘ 20ml overproof white rum
∘ blue food colouring
∘ 1 Campari Marshmallow *(see page 85)*
∘ pineapple leaves, to serve (optional)

1   Pour all the liquid ingredients except the white rum and food colouring into a cocktail shaker, add the ice cubes and shake well.
2   Strain the mixture into a tall glass. Separately mix the white rum with the food colouring. Turn a spoon upside down and hold it just above the level of the top of the cocktail, with its tip touching the glass. Slowly pour the coloured rum on to the back of the spoon. It should 'float', forming a blue layer on top of the orange drink.
3   Add a Campari marshmallow and gild the top of it slightly with a mini blowtorch. Arrange some pineapple leaves on top, if you like.

Winter, Home & Feasting

For me, winter is an endless pursuit of cosiness... Will there be red wine? Is there a fire? Should I bring a pair of gloves? Let's have some sausages! **... Will there be red wine?**

When there's a damp chill no layering of jumpers can defeat, you need food that blankets you in the familiar. Food that is soft, buttery and comforting. I crave cold days, grey with drizzle, when slow recipes are given much-warranted attention inside steamed-up kitchen windows.

Moving to London can be an exhilarating whirl of familiar sites, edgy happenings and limitless opportunity. But the city can also be exhaustingly big, prohibitively expensive and unnecessarily exclusive. On days when my opinion of the city is weighed down heavily by the latter, it's best for me to stay indoors and let London get on with itself.

Long meals that last until, or even start in, the early hours are what London winters are made for. Working in catering means that a lot of my friends finish or start shifts at irregular times, eat breakfast when most people would be thinking about dinner, or collapse around a table for raided-fridge feasts at 3am. In an attempt to bossily force normality and a bit of order on to others, I persistently organise communal meals; mostly sprawling Sunday dinners. For one day a week I want friends to trickle in, chairs to be in short supply and a rolling spread of courses to enjoy. I find it best to prepare desserts that can be made in advance so as to avoid mid-meal flaps, or to offer piles of individually portioned treats, ideal for overeating or place-hopping to join a new conversation. All of this is my favourite way to eat: when the food melts into the chat, then into more food, with elbows, shared spoons and spilled drinks.

Winter Marshmallow Recipes

1
Coconut

Follow the Whole Fruit Marshmallow recipe *(see page 15)*, but replace the fruit purée with 100ml good-quality coconut cream mixed with 90ml of water (the coconut cream is incredibly creamy and dense, so adding the water gives a light, fluffy texture). Once set and cut, roll the mallows in toasted desiccated coconut for a lovely crunch to contrast with their creamy texture. Double coconutty hit! To toast desiccated coconut, spread 100g of it evenly on a baking tray and cook in an oven preheated to 190°C/gas 5 for about 5 minutes. Keep a careful eye on this; it can catch *very* quickly.

2
Christmas Pudding

Follow the Whole Fruit Marshmallow recipe *(see page 15)*, but replace the fruit purée with 190ml of water. Use only 240g white granulated sugar but also add 50g dark muscovado sugar to give a deep caramel flavour. Add ¼ tsp cinnamon, ¼ tsp mixed spice and the grated zest of ½ orange to the mix. When the marshmallow is 2 minutes from pouring, add 2 tbsp brandy-soaked chopped dried mixed fruit.

4
Mulled Wine

Follow the Whole Fruit Marshmallow recipe *(see page 15)*, but replace the fruit purée with 190ml mulled wine and a pinch each of ground cinnamon and nutmeg.

3
Salted Caramel

Follow the Whole Fruit Marshmallow recipe *(see page 15)*, but replace the fruit purée with 100ml of water in the saucepan and 100ml Salted Caramel Sauce *(see page 126)* in the bowl of the stand mixer. Seconds before the marshmallow is ready to pour, swirl in 1 heaped tbsp Salted Caramel Sauce with the mixer on a low speed to add a delicious swirl to your mallow before pouring out.

Sticky Toffee Pudding with Vanilla Marshmallow Sauce

Serves 6–8

This is a very bossy pudding. It's the sort that turns up when you are absolutely stuffed at the end of a huge roast dinner – a long, boozy, two-different-sorts-of-potato roast dinner – and demands to be eaten. It doesn't care that you're full. It knows its gooey indulgence is flippin' well worth it, so pull yourself together and get a spoon, then drop and give me 20.

For the pudding

○ 60g unsalted butter, softened, plus more for the dish
○ 200g mixed chopped pitted dates and figs
○ 1 tsp bicarbonate of soda
○ 125g dark muscovado sugar
○ 150g soft dark brown sugar
○ 2 medium eggs, beaten
○ 175g self-raising flour
○ ½ tsp baking powder
○ pinch of mixed spice
○ ¼ tsp fine salt
○ 50g shelled walnuts

1 Preheat the oven to 180°C/gas 4 and butter a 24cm square baking dish.
2 Place the dates, figs and bicarb in a bowl and pour in 200ml of boiling water. Leave to soften until the water has been absorbed.
3 In the bowl of a stand mixer (or with a hand-held whisk) beat together the butter and both sugars until pale and fluffy. Gradually add the beaten eggs, little by little.
4 Sift the flour, baking powder, mixed spice and salt into the wet mixture and fold in using a wooden spoon. Once fully combined, add the soaked fruit, its soaking water and the walnuts. Mix through.
5 Pour the mixture into the prepared dish, smooth the top and bake in the preheated oven for 30–35 minutes, or until springy to the touch.

For the sauce

○ 150g unsalted butter
○ 150g soft brown sugar
○ 150g double cream
○ 100g Vanilla Bean Marshmallows (*see page 18*), chopped; set a couple aside to decorate

6 To make the sauce, place the butter, sugar and cream in a saucepan and whisk over a low heat until fully melted and dissolved. Bring to the boil, then reduce the heat and allow to simmer for 2–3 minutes until thick and gooey. Remove from the heat and stir in the mallows.
7 Poke holes in the surface of the still-hot cooked pudding with a sharp knife and pour the sauce over, allowing it to seep into the pudding. Cut into pieces and decorate each slice with a marshmallow.

Molten Chocolate Earl Grey Marshmallow Cakes

Makes 6

When I lived in Paris, I very quickly learned where to buy the 'favourite' of everything. Parisians are keen on 'favourites': the crustiest baguette; the ripest fruit; the chubbiest *choux* à *la crème*. I soon realised that Valrhona chocolate was my 'favourite'; it's used by all the best chocolatiers and it's the only chocolate I use in this rich, gooey dessert.

Handily, the batter for this can be prepared up to 8 hours before baking.

- 100g unsalted butter, chopped, plus more for the ramekins
- 200g dark Valrhona chocolate (70% cocoa solids), chopped
- 2 medium eggs, plus 2 egg yolks
- 110g caster sugar
- 35g plain flour, sifted
- 6 Earl Grey marshmallows (*see page 85*)
- cocoa powder, to dust

1   Butter 6 ramekins thoroughly so the cakes will pop out easily after cooking. If baking the cakes now, preheat the oven to 200°C/gas 6.

2   Weigh the chocolate and butter into a heatproof bowl and melt over a bain-marie (*see page 10*).

3   In a separate bowl, beat together the eggs, egg yolks and sugar until light and fluffy. Mix in the chocolate mixture, then lightly fold in the flour with a large metal spoon; avoid knocking out any air.

4   Spoon the mixture into the ramekins until halfway up the sides. Place an Earl Grey marshmallow into the centre of each and press it down lightly into the mixture. Pour the remaining chocolate mixture over the tops of the mallows. Don't overfill the ramekins, as the cakes will rise in the oven and you don't want them spilling over.

5   You can now place the pots in the fridge for up 8 hours. Just make sure you return them to room temperature before baking (leave them out of the fridge for 30 minutes) and preheat the oven to 200°C/gas 6.

6   Place the pots on a baking tray and bake in the hot oven for 16–18 minutes, or until the cakes spring back lightly when pressed. Carefully turn out on to plates, dust with cocoa powder and serve.

Elvis French Toast

Serves 8, or a hungry 4

There will come a time when, buoyed-yet-emotionally-broken by the success of my marshmallow empire, I will move to a remote estate in Memphis, Tennessee, hang up my rhinestone chef whites and zip around in a pink Cadillac. Perhaps then, while surveying my glimmering and extensive collection of bespoke whisks, I may fancy a sandwich. Not just any sandwich, as I'm sure you can imagine, but a sandwich created from thick, slightly sweet slabs of bread, sticky with unctuous peanut butter, slathered in smooth banana and embellished with smoky streaky b... Hold on, what? Someone already has? *Elvis*? Right, OK then. Fine.

So this self-indulgent 'Elvis-style' sandwich makes for a barn-storming winter breakfast. Although you can use any sliced white bread, I find it works best when using up the slightly stale leftovers from my Barterer's Brioche *(see page 98)*. The added sweetness of the vanilla bean marshmallow adds a decadence of which that Elvis fellow could only dream... *uh, huh, uh huh.*

For the sandwich

- 2 medium eggs, lightly beaten
- 100ml whole milk
- ½ tsp vanilla bean paste
- 50g caster sugar
- 1 tsp ground cinnamon
- pinch of grated nutmeg
- 8 slices of 2-day-old brioche *(see page 98 for home-made)*
- 50g unsalted butter

1   Preheat the oven to 170°C/gas 3½.
2   In a wide, shallow bowl mix the eggs, milk, vanilla, sugar and spices and whisk to combine. Soak the brioche slices in the egg mix for 30 seconds on each side.
3   In a large non-stick frying pan, melt a quarter of the butter (10–15g). When it starts to sizzle, place 2 brioche slices in the pan and fry for 2 minutes on each side until golden. Transfer to the oven to keep warm and cook the remaining brioche slices in batches of 2 in the same way, melting down portions of butter in between each.

To serve

- maple syrup, crispy bacon, chopped banana and 2 Vanilla Bean Marshmallows *(see page 27)* per serving

4   Drizzle with maple syrup and serve with crispy bacon, chopped banana and melted vanilla mallows on top. Or make the toppings into fillings for 4 killer sandwiches.

Marshmallow Brownies

Makes 10

When I was little I didn't want to join the Brownies... Nope, it wasn't for me. I yearned to be a Scout. To make fires, tie knots, play football. (I'm not sure if Scouts were allowed to play football. How would I know? I wasn't allowed to join.)

Thankfully, girls are now allowed to be Scouts. And, as it turns out, I make a really good brownie. But not that kind of Brownie.

Aided by the soft whip of marshmallow, these brownies are the perfect balance between the over-indulgent goo of some recipes and the tight cake crumb of others. They are definitely the sort of brownie you would award a badge to. A badge that one could, if one wished, sew on to a shirt sleeve.

○ 200g unsalted butter, chopped, plus more for the tin
○ 200g good-quality dark chocolate (70% cocoa solids), chopped
○ 5 medium eggs
○ 300g caster sugar
○ 125g plain flour
○ ½ tsp baking powder
○ pinch of salt
○ 200g shelled pecans, bashed into pieces
○ 150g Coconut Marshmallows *(see page 109)*, roughly chopped

1   Preheat the oven to 180°C/gas 4. Lightly butter a 25cm square baking tin and line with baking parchment. Melt the chocolate and butter in a bain-marie *(see page 10)*, stirring occasionally, then leave to cool for 5 minutes.

2   Meanwhile, beat together the eggs and sugar in a stand mixer (or with a hand-held whisk) until pale and mousse-like. This will take about 5 minutes.

3   Gently pour the melted chocolate into the egg and sugar mix and whisk lightly until combined. Sift in the flour, baking powder and salt, then fold lightly through with a large metal spoon.

4   Scatter the pecan pieces and chopped marshmallows over the prepared tin. Scrape in the brownie mix and smooth out. Bake in the preheated oven for 35–40 minutes, depending on how gooey you like your brownies; I recommend checking very frequently at this stage with the tip of a skewer.

5   Remove from the oven and leave in the tin to cool for at least 1 hour before cutting into squares.

Salted Caramel Marshmallow Cups

Makes 24

Taking inspiration from the perennially popular Reese's Peanut Butter Cups. I like to replace the peanut butter with a plump whip of freshly made Salted Caramel marshmallow and smother it in the almost savoury caramel before coating in chocolate.

The quantities given below for salted caramel sauce will make a large jar, but you will only need a quarter for this recipe. Use the remainder within 4 days, perhaps for my Millionaire's Marshmallows *(see page 130)*.

Equipment: 24 petits fours cases

∘ 75g unsalted butter
∘ 100g soft light brown sugar
∘ 1 tsp sea salt flakes (or more if you prefer it saltier), plus more to finish
∘ 125ml double cream

For the salted caramel sauce

1   Heat the butter, sugar and salt in a medium-sized heavy-based pan over a low heat, swirling the pan until all the sugar has fully dissolved. Let the mixture bubble away until it is a rich, light caramel colour, about 4 minutes or so. Be careful not to over-cook the caramel, otherwise it will burn and taste bitter.

2   Remove the pan from the heat and very gradually whisk in the cream, to avoid the caramel seizing up (and to avoid it spluttering up over your hands). Return to the heat for a further minute, then pour the sauce into a jug or a jar for storage. This will keep for 4 days in the fridge; if you do refrigerate it, warm it through slightly to soften it before using.

For the salted caramel marshmallow

○ 250g Salted
Caramel
Marshmallow
(*see page 109*)

3   To make salted caramel marshmallow, follow the recipe on p.109.

To assemble

○ 250g very good-quality
dark chocolate (70%
cocoa solids)
○ 24 petit four cases
(paper or foil)

4   Place 24 petits fours cases in a mini bun tin or mini tarte tin. Temper the chocolate over a bain-marie (*see opposite*).
5   Use a small paintbrush to coat the cases with tempered chocolate. Ensure that the base coating is quite thick and that the sides are fully covered. Leave to harden at room temperature: do not put in the fridge if you want your cups to have a glossy sheen.
6   Apply a second coat of tempered chocolate – it must be thick enough to avoid the caramel or marshmallow seeping out – and leave to harden at room temperature.
7   Using a small spoon (or a piping bag to be extra neat), dollop in the salted caramel sauce until each is three-quarters full. Spoon the caramel mallow over the top until the cups are completely filled.
8   When the mallow has set slightly, paint on the rest of the chocolate to seal. Sprinkle over salt flakes, then leave to harden.

How to temper chocolate

This just needs concentration and a good thermometer. It means slowly heating then cooling chocolate so the fats crystallise uniformly, enabling it to 'snap' rather than crumble. It gives a smooth, polished finish to home-made chocs and fortuitously raises the melting point, so you're less likely to get melted chocolate all over your hands while eating it. The slower you melt the chocolate, the better the result, so take your time and keep the heat very low.

You will need a thermometer, a bain marie, a bowl full of iced water and good quality dark chocolate chopped into smallish chunks.

1   Place chopped chocolate in a bowl set over a bain-marie (*see page 10*), ensuring the bowl doesn't touch the water. Gradually melt until it measures 55°C on a sugar thermometer, gently stirring all the time with a spatula. Remove the bowl from the heat and place over (not in) a bowl of iced water, reducing the temperature to 27°C.
2   Return the bowl to the bain-marie. Reheat to 31–32°C (ensure that the chocolate does not exceed 32°C). Use as instructed in the recipe.

Millionaire's Marshmallows

Makes 16

'This time next year, Rodney, we'll be...' ... still making Millionaire's Marshmallows, and eating them nonchalantly from the deck of your super yacht.

○ 100g unsalted butter, at room temperature, plus more for the tin
○ 150g plain flour
○ ½ tsp baking powder
○ 75g light brown muscovado sugar
○ 1 quantity Salted Caramel Sauce *(see page 126)*
○ 1 quantity Vanilla Bean Marshmallow *(see page 27)*
○ 200g good-quality dark chocolate (70% cocoa solids)
○ sea salt flakes, to sprinkle
○ edible gold leaf, to serve (optional)

1   Preheat the oven to 170°C/gas 3½. Butter a 20cm square cake tin and line with cling film.

2   To make the shortbread base, sift the flour, baking powder and sugar into a bowl. Rub in the butter with your fingertips, forming a buttery, sandy dough. Press this evenly into the base of the prepared tin and smooth it out with a spatula. Prick all over with a fork and bake for 30 minutes until golden. Leave to cool in the tin.

3   Pour the caramel sauce over the cooled shortbread and let it cool completely, about 45 minutes.

4   Spoon a thick layer of marshmallow over and chill in the fridge for 20 minutes. Meanwhile, temper the chocolate *(see page 129)*.

5   Pour the tempered chocolate over the mallow and smooth out evenly with a spatula. Sprinkle with sea salt and gold leaf, if using, then leave to set. Cut into squares (they will keep in the fridge for 3 days).

Chocolate Mousse with Mulled Wine Marshmallow

Serves 6

Chocolate and red wine make a pretty heady, love-struck couple. Once near a dessert, they only have eyes for each other.

'You hang up...'

'No, you hang up...'

[chocolate laughs coquettishly]

'No, you...'

○ 200g good-quality dark chocolate (70% cocoa solids)
○ 60g unsalted butter
○ 4 medium eggs, separated, plus
2 egg whites
○ 40g caster sugar
○ 6 Mulled Wine Marshmallows (*see page 109*)

1 Break the chocolate into pieces and place in a bowl with the butter to melt gently over a bain-marie (*see page 10*). Whisk the 4 egg yolks until very thick, then gently stir into the melted chocolate mixture.

2 In the bowl of a stand mixer, whisk the 6 egg whites into soft peaks, then add the sugar and whisk for a further 2 minutes until thick and glossy.

3 Remove the chocolate from the heat and beat in a third of the whisked egg white. Fold in another third of the egg white very gently, using a large metal spoon, until just combined. Lastly add the final third of whisked egg white, as softly as you possibly can: to keep your mousse light and fluffy, avoid over-mixing it.

4 Spoon the mousse into a large serving bowl and refrigerate for a few hours until set. Just before serving, place the mulled wine mallows on top and toast with a mini blowtorch until melting.

Marshmallowist's Popcorn

Serves 4

Roll up, roll up ladies and gentlemen, children of all ages...!
Behold, the best popcorn recipe in town. For one night only
I give you the incredible, the sweet, the maybe salty, the gooey
ex-tra-va-ganza that is Marshmallowist's Popcorn! *The crowd
goes wild...*

○ 500g popping corn
or microwave popcorn
○ 100g butter, salted
or unsalted
○ 100g brown sugar
○ 2 tbsp runny honey
○ 12 marshmallows, Vanilla
Bean works well, *(see page
27)* chopped

1   Pop the popcorn following the packet instructions and remove any
unpopped kernels. Place in a large bowl.
2   Put the butter in a medium-sized pan placed over a low heat with
the sugar, honey and marshmallows. Stir the mixture until all the
mallows are completely melted and smooth.
3   Pour the gooey mallow mixture over the bowl of popcorn and stir
until each kernel is evenly coated. Eat (or store in an airtight container
for up to 3 days).

Big Time Fun Cake

Serves 10–12

The sweet equivalent of a sequinned dress, a wad of cash and no fixed plans. It's a gigantic slice of swagger: 4 layers of chocolate sponge filled with chocolate ganache and fluffed marshmallow. Holla!

For the chocolate sponge

- unsalted butter, for the tins
- 350g plain flour, plus more to dust
- 600g caster sugar
- 125g good-quality cocoa powder
- 2 tbsp bicarbonate of soda
- 1 1/2 tsp baking powder
- 1 tsp salt
- 3 medium eggs, at room temperature (the cake won't rise properly otherwise)
- 360ml buttermilk
- 360ml freshly made strong coffee
- 180ml vegetable oil
- 1 tsp vanilla bean paste

1   To make the chocolate sponge, preheat the oven to 180°C/gas 4. Butter 2 × 24cm springform cake tins, line with baking parchment and dust lightly with flour, tapping out any excess.

2   Sift all the dry ingredients into the bowl of a stand mixer. In a measuring jug, beat together the eggs, buttermilk, coffee, oil and vanilla until lightly combined.

3   Pour the wet ingredients into the dry ingredients and mix on a medium speed for 2 minutes.

4   Divide the batter evenly between the prepared tins (don't worry that the layers are quite thin). Bake in the hot oven for 30–35 minutes or until a skewer comes out almost clean. Leave to cool in the tin for 30 minutes before turning out and cooling completely on a rack.

For the ganache

- 500g dark chocolate (70% cocoa solids), chopped small
- 500ml double cream
- 50g light brown muscovado sugar

5   To make the ganache, place the chopped chocolate in a heatproof bowl. Put the cream and sugar into a medium-sized pan and bring to a gentle simmer. Pour the heated cream over the chocolate, a third at a time, stirring until the chocolate has melted and the ganache is smooth and glossy. Set aside to cool.

To assemble

- 1 quantity Fluffed Marshmallow (see page 18)

6   Cut both cakes in half horizontally, using a long serrated bread knife, so you have 4 layers. Place a first layer of cake cut side up on a plate and cover generously with ganache. Place a second cake layer on top, cut side up, and cover with fluffed mallow; leave a good 2cm rim round the edge as the fluff smooshes out when you place the rest of the cake on top. Place a third cake layer on top and cover with chocolate ganache.

7   Alternate between ganache and marshmallow fillings until the final layer. Place the final layer cut-side down, so you have the most even surface on top.

8   Using the remaining ganache, pour it over the top of the cake and let it drip down the sides. Using a palette knife, smooth out the ganache until it forms a thin layer over all of the top and sides of the cake. Decorate with sparklers, gold leaf and smiles!

Ta very much...

To Rowan, Susannah and Rose at Square Peg for their enthusiasm and encouragement, for being unendingly patient and for creating such a stylish, individual and completely cherishable book. Especially to Susannah for overseeing all our wobbles of confidence with such calm assurance.

Imogen Pelham, at Marjacq for thinking that I could write a book, helping me with the book, not minding me moan about the book and generally being the boss of the book.

Jordanne, for making my marshmallows a 'thing'.

Carol Monpart for bringing such freshness, creative balance and edge to everything she touches. You have elevated the book to something more than recipes and musings.

The brilliant Helen Cathcart whose artistic vision has made this book so staggeringly gorgeous and whose efforts were above and beyond what we could have dreamed of in a photographer. You made the process feel collaborative, fun and I feel very privileged to have messed up your flat, stolen your pumpkin and got in the way of your light. To Linda Berlin for 'getting it' and providing each dish with its perfect backdrop.

To Leiths cookery school for providing such talented food assistants in Meghan Coker, Florence Cornish, Janet Chu and Johanne Keane.

To Cath Havercroft and The Communications Store for generously lending fresh-from-the-catwalk House of Holland clothes to play dress up in (and a huge thanks to ME for having the will power to give them back) To super stylist Elena Diaz for the dramatic make up, wild hair and lovely chats.

To all those who have helped shape and influence our design; the brilliant Veronica Lethorn, Matthew Scharf and G. F Smith for their beautifully produced papers, continued support and mentorship. To Eve Warren for her beautiful illustrations. James Taylor and Pression Print for producing beautiful backdrops at a moment's notice and Matthew Caddick at Chiswick auctions for the priceless eccentric props.

To Kim Galloway without whom the business would not be where it is today.

Finally, to Mum and Dad (Elf 1 and Elf 1A), John and Loz for their for their limitless patience and unwavering encouragement. You have been there for the early mornings, late endings, long drives and impossible deadlines and we love you very much.

1 3 5 7 9 10 8 6 4 2

Square Peg, an imprint of Vintage,
 20 Vauxhall Bridge Road,
London SW1V 2SA

Square Peg is part of the Penguin Random House group
of companies whose addresses can be found at global.
penguinrandomhouse.com.

First published by Square Peg in 2016

www.penguin.co.uk/vintage

A CIP catalogue record for this book is available from the
British Library

ISBN 9780224100991

Design by Carol Montpart
Photography by Helen Cathcart
Props by Linda Berlin

Printed and bound by Toppan Leefung Printing Limited